DISCARD

Families Today

MULTIRACIAL FAMILIES

Families Today

Adoptive Families

Disability and Families

Foster Families

Homelessness and Families

Immigrant Families

Incarceration and Families

LGBT Families

Military Families

Multigenerational Families

Multiracial Families

Single-Parent Families

Teen Parents

Families Today

MULTIRACIAL FAMILIES

H.W. Poole

MASON CREST

Mason Crest
450 Parkway Drive, Suite D
Broomall, PA 19008
www.masoncrest.com

© 2017 by Mason Crest, an imprint of National Highlights, Inc. All rights reserved. No part of this publication may be reproduced or transmitted in any form or by any means, electronic or mechanical, including photocopying, recording, taping, or any information storage and retrieval system, without permission from the publisher.

MTM Publishing, Inc.
435 West 23rd Street, #8C
New York, NY 10011
www.mtmpublishing.com

President: Valerie Tomaselli
Vice President, Book Development: Hilary Poole
Designer: Annemarie Redmond
Copyeditor: Peter Jaskowiak
Editorial Assistant: Andrea St. Aubin

Series ISBN: 978-1-4222-3612-3
Hardback ISBN: 978-1-4222-3622-2
E-Book ISBN: 978-1-4222-8266-3

Library of Congress Cataloging-in-Publication Data
Names: Poole, Hilary W., author.
Title: Multiracial families / by H.W. Poole.
Description: Broomall, PA : Mason Crest [2017] | Series: Families Today | Includes index.
Identifiers: LCCN 2016004551| ISBN 9781422236222 (hardback) | ISBN 9781422236123 (series) | ISBN 9781422282663 (e-book)
Subjects: LCSH: Racially mixed families—Juvenile literature. | Interracial marriage—Juvenile literature. | Racially mixed children—Juvenile literature. | Interracial adoption—Juvenile literature. | Families—Juvenile literature.
Classification: LCC HQ1031 .P63 2017 | DDC 306.84/6—dc23
LC record available at http://lccn.loc.gov/2016004551

Printed and bound in the United States of America.

First printing
9 8 7 6 5 4 3 2 1

TABLE OF CONTENTS

Series Introduction 7
Chapter One: What Is a Multiracial Family? 11
Chapter Two: Interracial Relationships 17
Chapter Three: Transracial Adoption 27
Chapter Four: A Multiracial Life 37
Further Reading 44
Series Glossary 45
Index 47
About the Author 48
Photo Credits 48

Key Icons to Look for:

Words to Understand: These words with their easy-to-understand definitions will increase the reader's understanding of the text, while building vocabulary skills.

Sidebars: This boxed material within the main text allows readers to build knowledge, gain insights, explore possibilities, and broaden their perspectives by weaving together additional information to provide realistic and holistic perspectives.

Research Projects: Readers are pointed toward areas of further inquiry connected to each chapter. Suggestions are provided for projects that encourage deeper research and analysis.

Text-Dependent Questions: These questions send the reader back to the text for more careful attention to the evidence presented there.

Series Glossary of Key Terms: This back-of-the-book glossary contains terminology used throughout the series. Words found here increase the reader's ability to read and comprehend higher-level books and articles in this field.

In the 21st century, families are more diverse than ever before.

SERIES INTRODUCTION

Our vision of "the traditional family" is not nearly as time-honored as one might think. The standard of a mom, a dad, and a couple of kids in a nice house with a white-picket fence is a relic of the 1950s—the heart of the baby boom era. The tumult of the Great Depression followed by a global war caused many Americans to long for safety and predictability—whether such stability was real or not. A newborn mass media was more than happy to serve up this image, in the form of TV shows like *Leave It To Beaver* and *The Adventures of Ozzie and Harriet*. Interestingly, even back in the "glory days" of the traditional family, things were never as simple as they seemed. For example, a number of the classic "traditional" family shows—such as *The Andy Griffith Show, My Three Sons,* and a bit later, *The Courtship of Eddie's Father*—were actually focused on single-parent families.

Sure enough, by the 1960s our image of the "perfect family" was already beginning to fray at the seams. The women's movement, the gay rights movement, and—perhaps more than any single factor—the advent of "no fault" divorce meant that the illusion of the Cleaver family would become harder and harder to maintain. By the early 21st century, only about 7 percent of all family households were traditional—defined as a married couple with children where *only* the father works outside the home.

As the number of these traditional families has declined, "nontraditional" arrangements have increased. There are more single parents, more gay and lesbian parents, and more grandparents raising grandchildren than ever before. Multiracial families—created either through interracial relationships or adoption—are also increasing. Meanwhile, the transition to an all-volunteer military force has meant that there are more kids growing up in military families than there were in the past. Each of these topics is treated in a separate volume in this set.

While some commentators bemoan the decline of the traditional family, others argue that, overall, the recognition of new family arrangements has brought more good than bad. After all, if very few people live like the Cleavers anyway, isn't it better to be honest about that fact? Surely, holding up the traditional family as an ideal to which all should aspire only serves to stigmatize kids whose lives differ from that standard. After all, no children can be held responsible for whatever family they find themselves in; all they can do is grow up as best they can. These books take the position that every family—no matter what it looks like—has the potential to be a successful family.

That being said, challenges and difficulties arise in every family, and nontraditional ones are no exception. For example, single parents tend to be less well off financially than married parents are, and this has long-term impacts on their children. Meanwhile, teenagers who become parents tend to let their educations suffer, which damages their income potential and career possibilities, as well as risking the future educational attainment of their babies. There are some 400,000 children in the foster care system at any given time. We know that the uncertainty of foster care creates real challenges when it comes to both education and emotional health.

Furthermore, some types of "nontraditional" families are ones we wish did not have to exist at all. For example, an estimated 1.6 million children experience homelessness at some point in their lives. At least 40 percent of homeless kids are lesbian, gay, bisexual, or transgender teens who were turned out of their homes because of their orientation. Meanwhile, the United States incarcerates more people than any other nation in the world—about 2.7 million kids (1 in 28) have an incarcerated parent. It would be absurd to pretend that such situations are not extremely stressful and, often, detrimental to kids who have to survive them.

The goal of this set, then, is twofold. First, we've tried to describe the history and shape of various nontraditional families in such a way that kids who aren't familiar with them will be able to not only understand, but empathize. We also present demographic information that may be useful for students who are dipping their toes into introductory sociology concepts.

Second, we have tried to speak specifically to the young people who are living in these nontraditional families. The series strives to address these kids as

Meeting challenges and overcoming them together can make families stronger.

sympathetically and supportively as possible. The volumes look at some of the typical problems that kids in these situations face, and where appropriate, they offer advice and tips for how these kids might get along better in whatever situation confronts them.

Obviously, no single book—whether on disability, the military, divorce, or some other topic—can hope to answer every question or address every problem. To that end, a "Further Reading" section at the back of each book attempts to offer some places to look next. We have also listed appropriate crisis hotlines, for anyone with a need more immediate than can be addressed by a library.

Whether your students have a project to complete or a problem to solve, we hope they will be able to find clear, empathic information about nontraditional families in these pages.

—H. W. Poole

Multiracial Families

Bill de Blasio with his family—wife Chirlane McCray, daughter Chiara, and son Dante—at a civil rights march in New York City in 2012.

Chapter One

WHAT IS A MULTIRACIAL FAMILY?

When Bill de Blasio was sworn in as mayor of New York City on January 1, 2015, the moment was significant for several reasons. For one thing, the election of de Blasio, a Democrat, was a political change for the city. But for many people around the country, de Blasio's victory represented something more personal. De Blasio is white, his wife, Chirlane McCray, is black, and together they have two biracial children, Chiara and Dante. This made de Blasio the first white politician with a black spouse to be elected to a major office in the

Words to Understand

census: a survey of a particular population.

demographers: people who study information about people and communities.

ethnicity: a group that has a shared cultural heritage.

transracial: involving more than one race; across racial lines.

12 Multiracial Families

United States. A multiracial family would now occupy the mayor's residence of America's largest city.

MAKING A MULTIRACIAL FAMILY

How are multiracial families made? There are two main ways. The first is when two people of different racial backgrounds fall in love. They are usually referred to as an interracial couple, and any children they have together would be considered biracial or multiracial. Similarly, someone might marry, have children, divorce, and then remarry. If the new spouse is of a different race, this situation also creates a biracial or multiracial family.

The second major way that multiracial families are made is when a person or couple adopts a child who has a different racial background. So, for example, two white parents might adopt a black or Asian child. This is called **transracial** adoption, because *trans* means "across," and a transracial adoption takes place across racial lines.

Hispanic Origin

When filling out a form—on a standardized test, for example—you might notice that there is one question about your race, and a separate one about "Hispanic origin." Some people find this confusing, because they think of someone who is "Latino" as being a different race from a white, black, or Asian person. But in fact the term *Hispanic* includes a huge range of individuals, and people of Hispanic **ethnicity** can be of different races. Latinos can be white or black, or neither, or both! That's why the question about Hispanic origin is often listed separately.

This may be changing, however. The U.S. Census Bureau revised the ethnicity question for its 2010 count, and it is likely to do so again for the next census in 2020.

Chapter One: What Is a Multiracial Family?

> I am the son of a black man from Kenya and a white woman from Kansas.... I have brothers, sisters, nieces, nephews, uncles, and cousins, of every race and every hue, scattered across three continents, and for as long as I live, I will never forget that in no other country on Earth is my story even possible.
>
> —U.S. President Barack Obama, 2008

The Obama family on election night, 2008.

There are two types of adoption: domestic and international. A domestic U.S. adoption involves a child already in the United States, while an international one involves bringing a child from another country to the United States.

COUNTING MULTIRACIAL FAMILIES

In the 2010 **census**, more than 9 million Americans described themselves as being of more than one race. This group includes celebrities such as the musicians Drake and Rihanna, the actors Halle Berry and Dwayne "The Rock" Johnson, and athletes such as Derek Jeter, Gabrielle Reece, Carmelo Anthony, and Tiger Woods. And let's not forget President Barack Obama, who is the son of a white mother and black father.

Demographers say the number of people who identify as two different races (biracial) or more than two (multiracial) will continue to grow. In fact, some

Multiracial Families

INTERRACIAL/INTERETHNIC MARRIED-COUPLE HOUSEHOLDS IN THE UNITED STATES

	Number	Percent
Total Interracial/Interethnic Couples	5,369,035	100
Non-Hispanic White/Hispanic (any race)	2,020,825	37.6
Non-Hispanic White/Non-Hispanic Black	422,250	7.9
Non-Hispanic White/Non-Hispanic American Indian and Alaska Native	280,780	5.2
Non-Hispanic White/Non-Hispanic Asian	737,493	13.7
One Partner Reporting Multiple Races*	838,190	15.6
Both Partners Reporting Multiple Races*	341,255	6.4
Hispanic/Non-Hispanic	390,650	7.3

*Includes Hispanic and non-Hispanic.
Source: U.S. Census Bureau, "Mapping Interracial/Interethnic Married-Couple Households in the United States: 2010." https://www.census.gov/hhes/socdemo/marriage/data/census/InterracialMarriages_PAA2013_FINAL.pdf.

experts predict that the number of bi- or multiracial people will increase by almost 200 percent by 2050. That's a far larger increase than is predicted for any single race or ethnicity.

Given this increase, it makes sense that the number of bi- or multiracial couples are growing, too. In the 2010 census, 5.4 percent of married couples described themselves as "interracial." That's a 28 percent increase from the previous census in 2000. Unmarried couples living together reported an even higher number of interracial relationships: about 18 percent of unmarried couples are of different races or Hispanic backgrounds. Overall, interracial couples make up just under 10 percent of the U.S. population.

A GROWING MINORITY

Since the 1980s, there has been more than a 400 percent increase in the number of marriages between white and black people. But that's nothing compared to

Chapter One: What Is a Multiracial Family?

marriages between white and Asian people—intermarriage between these groups has increased 1,000 times in the past 35 years.

Still, multiracial families are a small percentage of the overall number of U.S. families. As seen in the accompanying table, there were about 5.4 million interracial or interethnic married-couple households in the 2010 census. But that's actually not as big a number as it might sound—the census reported more than 56.5 million married-couple households overall. So interracial/interethnic households are a bit less than 10 percent of the total, or still very much a minority.

Being a multiracial family presents some unique challenges in day-to-day life. But it also offers unique opportunities.

Text-Dependent Questions

1. Who was the first white politician to be elected to a major U.S. office while married to a person of a different race?
2. By what percentage did the number of interracial relationships increase between the years 2000 and 2010? What was the percentage difference between married and unmarried couples?
3. Use the table on page 14 to figure out the most common type of interracial or interethnic married couple in the United States.

Research Project

Look up the 2010 census online and explore the various statistics about multiracial families. What can you learn about these families live? For example, see if you can figure out where they are most likely to live, or what kind of education they are most likely to have. (See https://www.census.gov/prod/cen2010/briefs/c2010br-14.pdf.)

16 Multiracial Families

Richard and Mildred Loving, who defied their state's law against interracial marriage.

Chapter Two

INTERRACIAL RELATIONSHIPS

It was the middle of the night on June 11, 1958. Richard and Mildred Loving were sound asleep in their home. They were woken by three policemen, shining flashlights in their eyes. The couple were arrested and taken to the police station in Central Point, Virginia. Richard Loving was kept in jail for a day, while Mildred was kept there for five. They were eventually convicted and each sentenced to a year in prison.

Words to Understand

abolitionists: people who worked to end slavery.

apartheid: a political system based on the idea that the races should be kept separate.

genetics: biological process that controls inherited physical traits.

ideology: a set of ideas and ways of seeing the world.

miscegenation: an old term for interracial relationships, especially marriage; the term implies criticism of these relationships.

prejudice: prejudging; a set of beliefs about a person or group based only on simplified and often mistaken ideas.

Had they robbed a bank? Burned down someone's house? Run over someone with their car? No. They had gotten married. That was their crime. Richard Loving was white, and his wife was black and Native American. In Virginia—and in 15 other U.S. states at the time—marriage between people of different races was illegal.

SCIENCE AND RACE

In one sense, we all know what the word *race* means. Some people have darker skin, some have lighter. Some are of Asian descent, some are of Native American descent, and so on. It all seems pretty obvious. But there is nothing "obvious" about race.

The officers who arrested Richard and Mildred Loving probably believed—as many people did at the time—that there were huge differences between people with different shades of skin. But thanks to a better understanding of **genetics**, we now know this is not true. The genetic differences between people of different races are in fact very tiny. Indeed, there are more genetic differences between girls and boys of the same race than there are between people of different races. On a biological level, the concept of race has no meaning.

But don't tell Mildred Loving, who spent five days in a rat-infested jail simply because she'd married a white man, that race doesn't mean anything. Clearly it meant, and means, a lot.

HISTORY AND RACE

If race has no scientific basis, where does it come from?

In ancient societies, people were rarely divided by their physical characteristics. Ancient Greeks tended to see the world as divided between Greeks and everyone else. "Race," as we think of it today, was not part of their thought process. Any person could be considered Greek, regardless of skin color, as long as he learned the language and participated in Greek society.

Chapter Two: Interracial Relationships

The genetic differences between different races are almost nonexistent.

In fact, the word *race* isn't even very old. It dates back to the 16th century, when race meant "having common ancestors." Even then, the word didn't necessarily refer to skin color. This is not to say that people didn't prejudge each other in the past. Humans have always tended to prefer people of their own group over outsiders (see sidebar). But *race* and *racism* as we know it are far more recent inventions.

In the late 1600s, when America was little more than an experiment, a lot of people traveled to the colonies to work. Some came willingly—they were called *indentured servants*. These servants agreed to work for a set period of time. When that time ended, they could go do what they wanted. But other workers did not come to America willingly at all. They were captured, usually in Africa, and forced to come as slaves.

At first, no major distinctions were made between servants and slaves. They worked together, socialized together, and even intermarried. But this situation

Ancient Prejudice

The idea of race may be fairly new, but **prejudice** is as old as humanity itself. Consider this passage from Aristotle, the ancient Greek philosopher:

> Those who live in a cold climate and in Europe are full of spirit, but wanting in intelligence and skill; and therefore they ... are incapable of ruling over others. Whereas the natives of Asia are intelligent and inventive, but they are wanting in spirit, and therefore they are always in a state of subjection and slavery. But the [Greeks, who are] ... situated between them, [are] likewise intermediate in character, being high-spirited and also intelligent. Hence [Greece] continues free, and is the best-governed of any nation, and if it could be formed into one state, would be able to rule the world.

Notice how Aristotle stereotypes large groups of people, based only on where they were born. Then he turns these stereotypes into an argument for why one group—his group!—should be in charge of everyone else.

You can still hear these same sorts of beliefs today, when people talk about racism. People tell themselves that one group is "naturally" better than the other, and they use this false belief to excuse all kinds of terrible actions.

A statue of Aristotle at his birthplace, in Stageira, Greece.

Chapter Two: Interracial Relationships

The memorial sculpture *Memory for the Slaves* by Clara Sörnäs at the Stone Town Slave Market in Zanzibar.

did not last long. The Virginia colony banned interracial marriages in 1691, and other colonies soon followed. As the colonies grew, the need for labor also grew. Businessmen realized that indentured servants were not very reliable. They would always leave after completing their contracts, and the businessmen then had to find more workers. Slaves, who by definition could not leave, were viewed as more desirable. This was when race became more important.

RACE AS AN IDEA

As more and more people were kidnapped from their homes in Africa, the concept of *slavery* became associated with people from that part of the world. In other words, the term *slave* did not initially mean *African*. Over time, however, people began to see it that way. And if one group is considered inferior to another, then it is easier for people to accept that group being treated unfairly. An **ideology** of white superiority was used to explain why some people could be forced into slavery.

Multiracial Families

The United States was founded on principles of equality. In 1776 the Declaration of Independence stated this clearly: "We hold these truths to be self-evident, that all men are created equal...." But if this was true, how could slavery be justified? There were many people, even at that time, who knew that slavery was immoral and wrong. Also in 1776, the author and **abolitionist** Thomas Day wrote, "If there be an object truly ridiculous in nature, it is an American patriot, signing [the Declaration] with one hand, and with the other brandishing a whip over his affrighted slaves." Unfortunately, the vast majority of whites wanted slavery to continue: some people were proslavery because it was good for them financially; many others simply believed the lie of white supremacy.

Throughout the 18th and 19th centuries, abolitionists worked hard to convince people that slavery was wrong. It took a long time. The state of Pennsylvania abolished slavery in 1780, and other northern states followed. But it took almost another hundred years before slavery in the United States was ended once and for all. Unfortunately, the ideology that excused slavery has

A "Europeans only" bench in Johannesburg, South Africa, in 1972. On the right it says "whites only" in the language of Afrikaans.

Chapter Two: Interracial Relationships

Frederick Douglass

Frederick Douglass was a prominent abolitionist, a friend of Abraham Lincoln, and a former slave himself. He wrote and spoke powerfully to convince his fellow Americans to rise up and end slavery. In the 1852 speech called "What to the Slave Is the Fourth of July?," he said:

> At a time like this, scorching irony, not convincing argument, is needed.... It is not light that is needed, but fire; it is not the gentle shower, but thunder. We need the storm, the whirlwind, and the earthquake. The feeling of the nation must be quickened; the conscience of the nation must be roused; the propriety of the nation must be startled; the hypocrisy of the nation must be exposed; and its crimes against God and man must be proclaimed and denounced.

Portrait of Frederick Douglass.

not gone away. Elements of that same ideology persist, except we call it *white supremacy* or simply *racism*.

These ideas have not only been used against African Americans. The myth of white supremacy was also used to justify taking lands from Native Americans and Mexicans. It has also been used to justify limits on who can immigrate to the United States. For example, the Chinese Exclusion Act of 1882 existed solely to keep one group of people out of the country. The ideology of white supremacy is certainly not limited to the United States, either. Elements can be found in the philosophy of the Nazi regime in Germany, and in the **apartheid** system that existed in South Africa until 1994.

RACE AND RELATIONSHIPS

It was racism that sent Richard and Mildred Loving to jail on that dark night in 1958. The Lovings had broken a law against **miscegenation**—specifically, a Virginia law that banned relationships between people of different races. As mentioned earlier, laws against interracial relationships go back all the way to colonial times.

The judge in the Lovings' case declared, "Almighty God created the races… and he placed them on separate continents. The fact that he separated the races

The *Loving v. Virginia* case paved the way for future multiracial families.

shows that he did not intend for the races to mix." The judge sentenced the Lovings to one year in prison. But he said the couple could avoid jail time if they agreed to leave Virginia and not come back.

After initially agreeing to the judge's instructions, the Lovings changed their minds and pursued legal action. Their case went all the way to the U.S. Supreme Court. In 1967 the Court declared antimiscegenation laws to be unconstitutional. The ruling in the case, known as *Loving v. Virginia*, permanently changed our understanding of what makes a family.

Text-Dependent Questions

1. What was the original meaning of the word *race*?
2. What are some of the historical reasons behind the ideology of white supremacy?
3. What was the Supreme Court case that declared antimiscegenation laws to be unconstitutional?

Research Project

Find out more about the abolitionist movement. Make a timeline that begins with Pennsylvania's abolition of slavery in 1780 and ends with the Thirteenth Amendment to the U.S. Constitution in 1865. What were some of the key events that led from one to the other?

Author and transracial adoption advocate Pearl Buck.

Chapter Three

TRANSRACIAL ADOPTION

Pearl Buck was born in Hillsboro, West Virginia, in 1892. Her parents were **missionaries** in China, and Pearl spent much of her life there. She developed a great love for and understanding of Chinese culture, but she also understood very well what it was like to be an outsider. She used all these experiences as a writer; her book *The Good Earth* (1931) won many awards and is considered a classic.

A celebrity of her day, Buck used her fame for a good cause: helping to arrange adoptions for Asian and biracial orphans. When American soldiers were stationed overseas for long periods of time, they sometimes had relationships with local women, which resulted in the birth of biracial children. But these

---

Words to Understand

diverse: having variety; for example, "ethnically diverse" means a group of people of many different ethnicities.

infertile: unable to conceive a baby.

missionaries: people sent to foreign countries to convert others to their religion.

children were often not wanted by their communities, nor were they welcome in the United States. After hearing these children described as "unadoptable" just because of their race, Pearl Buck founded Welcome House in 1949. Welcome House was the first transracial adoption agency, and it has helped arrange adoptions for more than 7,000 orphans from 28 countries.

This was not just charity work to Buck: she adopted seven children and raised them as her own. In 1972 she wrote about her personal experiences with transracial adoption:

> *It has been a rich experience and it continues to be. It has brought me into the whole world.... I would not have missed the interesting experience of adopting children of races different than my own. They have taught me much. They have stretched my mind and heart. They have brought me, through love, into kinship with peoples different from my own ... ancestry.*

DOMESTIC ADOPTION

Why do people adopt? There are almost as many reasons as there are adoptive parents. Sometimes couples are **infertile**, and so they decide to expand their family through adoption instead. Many gay and lesbian couples who want to be parents choose to adopt. Sometimes a single person might want

Counting Transracial Adoptions

All adopted children in the United States were counted as part of the 2010 census, which found more than 400,000 transracially adopted children under the age of 18—that's about 40 percent of all adoptions. The most common ethnic background of the children was Hispanic, followed by Asian, bi- or multiracial, and African American.

Chapter Three: Transracial Adoption

to become a parent without waiting around for the perfect partner. And some families don't "need" to adopt but choose to do so, simply because they want to expand their families.

Once a person or couple decides to adopt, a number of questions must be asked. Where will their new child come from? Does it have to be an infant, or might they consider adopting an older child? Would they adopt a child with special needs? Or from another country? And then, often, there is the question of race and ethnicity.

Laws regarding gay and lesbian adoptions vary by state and are still evolving.

Even after the Loving case made intermarriage legal, transracial domestic adoptions were still controversial. For many years, adoption policy was guided by a concept called "matching." This is the idea that adopted kids should look just like their new parents, or "match" them. Adopted children were expected to basically disappear into their new families—perhaps never even knowing they were adopted at all. Of course, if parents and children are of different races, this is impossible.

A lot has changed over the years. Adoptions used to be "closed," meaning that the adoptive parents and the biological mother never knew each other. Many people no longer believe that this level of secrecy is necessary. According to the Evan B. Donaldson Adoption Institute, about two-thirds of adoptive families now have some contact with the biological mother of their adopted child. As

Multiracial Families

The Multiethnic Placement Act was passed by Congress in 1994 to encourage transracial adoptions.

the idea of "openness" in adoptions has become more accepted, it has also gotten easier for people to accept adoptions between people who do not "match" each other racially.

In fact, since the 1980s, children have been transracially adopted in increasing numbers. In 1994, Congress passed the Multiethnic Placement Act, which had three goals: (1) to decrease the amount of time children had to wait for adoption; (2) to actively recruit more **diverse** families who might adopt children; and (3) to end racial discrimination in adoption. The act prohibits adoption agencies from delaying adoptions for reasons of race. As the statistics above show, domestic transracial adoptions are becoming more common all the time. However, some

Chapter Three: Transracial Adoption

Case Study: Chakori

Chakori has two white parents, two brown sisters, and a white brother. She and her two younger sisters, Daya and Prisha, were born in India. Chakori was five years old when her mother died. "She was very beautiful," Chakori says. "I remember the colors of her saris, the way they felt against my cheek, the way she smelled.... The next thing I really remember is the orphanage."

Chakori still feels connected to her racial heritage. "We live in a community where there are lots of brown people," she explains. "My two best friends are both Indian, though they were born in the United States. Our families like to hang out together, and their moms have taught my mom how to cook real Indian food." Chakori and her family have traveled to India, and they visited the orphanage where the girls once lived. "We came back with suitcases filled with saris and bangles," she says. "Mom and the girls and I had such fun shopping."

But mostly Chakori feels like a member of her own, American family. "I can't imagine not belonging to this family. Mom, Dad, Luke, Daya, and Prisha—we're a unit. We belong together. That's what a real family is: people who love each other, whose identities and memories are all mixed up together."

—adapted from *Multiracial Families* by Julianna Fields (Mason Crest, 2010)

people still believe that children do best when adopted by parents who are of the same race or ethnicity (see below).

INTERNATIONAL ADOPTION

The adoption of foreign orphans by American parents began after World War II. Wars and catastrophes have frequently sparked increases in international adoptions. For example, the first major wave of international adoptions happened after the Korean War (1950–1953). The 1991 collapse of the Soviet Union into its various components (including Russia, Romania, Poland, and so on) sparked another rise in adoptions, and the AIDS crisis in the late 1980s and 1990s led to many adoptions from African countries. But it was the trend of celebrities adopting kids from developing countries that really brought the practice to the media's attention. Stars like Madonna and Angelina Jolie adopted multiple children from different countries.

Between 1999 and 2013 in the United States, there were 250,000 children adopted from other countries. From 2002 to 2006, in particular, more than 20,000 children were adopted from other countries each year. The two most common countries were China and Ethiopia, and other popular countries for adoption were South Korea and Guatemala.

This means that a great many international adoptions are also transracial; one study found the total to be about 80 percent. According to the U.S. census, in 2010 there were 123,000 kids under 18 who had been adopted from countries in Asia, just under 50,000 from countries in Central and South America, and about

Illegal Adoptions

In one sense, international adoptions can be viewed as a very generous thing. Parents take an orphan from a poor or struggling country and give that child a new life in the United States. Unfortunately, the situation is not always quite that simple.

In 2009, for example, 16 people in Vietnam were on trial for selling more than 250 babies. Because of such incidents, it is very important that international adoptions are closely monitored, and that would-be parents take care to only adopt from highly reputable agencies.

Chapter Three: Transracial Adoption

Orphans from the Maison Des Enfants de Dieu orphanage in Haiti on their way to meet their adoptive parents in the United States, in 2010.

10,000 from countries in Africa. Of all these adopted kids, the census reported that about 158,000 were of racial backgrounds different from their new parents, and about 44,000 were of different Hispanic ethnicities.

OBJECTIONS TO TRANSRACIAL ADOPTIONS

The practice of transracial adoption has some critics. Complaints from racists—people who don't believe that the races should mix at all—are the easiest to dismiss. Love is love, and good parents will protect and nurture their kids no matter what their race might be.

But some concerns about transracial adoptions can't be waved away so easily. In 1972 the National Association of Black Social Workers (NABSW) took a strong stand against the practice. They described it as "unnatural," and called for "Black

Multiracial Families

families for Black children." The NABSW feared that African-American children with white parents would grow up without a sense of their culture. They also argued that no matter how loving a white home might be, the children would not be prepared to cope with the racism that would greet them outside the home.

Critics also worried about children of color being yanked away from their own communities to be raised in a supposedly better—but really just whiter—environment. Native American activists have raised the same concern. Unfortunately, there is a long history of Native American children being forcibly taken from their families to be raised as "white." The Indian Child Welfare Act of 1978 rightly made this practice illegal. But some activists say that it still takes place.

Over time, most objections to transracial adoption have softened. Most people now agree that the first order of business is to get orphaned kids into stable

According to the U.S. Department of Health and Human Services, 40 percent of adoptions are transracial.

Chapter Three: Transracial Adoption

homes—regardless of what race that home might be. But experts also agree that it's very important that parents respect the birth culture of their adopted children. Parents should not pretend to be "color blind." Instead, they should encourage kids to feel proud about who they truly are.

Text-Dependent Questions

1. What are the different ways adoption can create multiracial families?
2. What are some criticisms of interracial adoptions? What do you think about these criticisms?
3. What approach should adoptive parents take to help their kids grow up well adjusted?

Research Project

Use U.S. census data to create a map that shows trends in adoption. For example, you could make a map that shows the numbers of adopted kids in each U.S. region or state. Or you could use data about international adoptions to make a world map that shows what countries adopted kids come from. These data are available from the Census Bureau—see the publication "Adopted Children and Stepchildren: 2010," available online at https://www.census.gov/prod/2014pubs/p20-572.pdf.

36 Multiracial Families

The more common multiracial families become, the more frequently you will see advertisements that cater to them.

Chapter Four

A MULTIRACIAL LIFE

It was, in most ways, a standard TV commercial. An adorable little girl approaches her mother with a box of cereal. The two discuss the health benefits of the cereal. Then we see the father wake up from a nap, only to find that his daughter has poured the entire box of cereal all over him. The screen fades to the cereal's logo and the jingle plays. That was the end of the commercial. But it was not, as it turned out, the end of the story.

The mother in the 2013 commercial was white, the father was black, and their daughter was biracial. And the outcry over the ad was so intense that the company, General Mills, shut down the comments section on the commercial's YouTube page. General Mills later clarified that there were many more positive

Words to Understand

extended family: the kind of family that includes members beyond just parents and children, such as aunts, uncles, cousins, and so on.
integrate: to weave two or more things together.
paradox: a statement or situation that seems to contradict itself.

comments than negative ones, but that the negative ones were so ugly that they decided it was better to disable the comments.

In response, a campaign was started called "We Are the Fifteen Percent," in which multiracial families posted photos of themselves online. The multiracial cereal family returned to television the following year, when a sequel to the first ad appeared in a key spot during the 2014 Super Bowl.

MIXING CULTURES

A big question for kids in multiracial families is simply, "Where do I fit in?" Mixed-race kids often look somewhat different from both of their parents—a child with white and black parents might have light skin but kinky hair, for example, or darker skin but smoother hair. Biracial kids often don't look exactly "white" or exactly "black," "Asian," or "Hispanic," either. Genetically, they are an equal part of both groups, but physically they stand out wherever they go. This is a real **paradox** that can be painful for biracial kids to experience. A kid with a black mom and a white dad can *feel* that he or she is a part of both cultures, but outsiders might judge that kid to be "not black enough" to be African American, but also "not white enough" to be Caucasian.

Transracially adopted kids often experience the same feelings, but on a cultural level. For example, a child born in South Korea but raised by white parents

> When you have a transracial family, mixed-race family, you're going outside the normal. Somebody has to be uncomfortable and it shouldn't be the child. . . . Your child should not be your first black friend. That's the bottom line.
>
> —Chad Goller-Sojourner, an African American who was adopted by white parents

Chapter Four: A Multiracial Life

Some biracial kids don't look exactly like one of their parents. That can sometimes result in some ignorant questions. Experts suggest using these moments as opportunities to teach other people about how every mixed-race child is unique.

might *look* just like any other Asian kid, but she or he may *feel* more at home in a white environment than in an Asian one. It can take years for adoptees to **integrate** their birth culture with the culture in which they were raised.

These feelings often evolve over time. It's normal for kids to develop a greater curiosity about their ethnic backgrounds as they grow into teenagers and young adults. Multiracial kids and adoptees may experiment with identifying with one or the other culture for a time. It can be very helpful to seek out other kids and families who are also multiracial or multicultural. Support from people who have been in the same situation can be a big help.

Multiracial Families

As teenagers, it's common for kids to be drawn to friends who share their ethnic backgrounds.

According to parenting experts, the more parents can do to expose their kids to all aspects of their background, the better off the kids will be. The days of "matching" and "colorblindness" are over. Experts advise parents to be "color conscious" instead. They frequently advise parents to celebrate diversity in their families: observe different holidays, explore new traditions, and spend time with people of different ethnic backgrounds. Rather than shying away from the "multi-" part of a multiracial family, think of it as a strength instead.

DEALING WITH RACISM

It would be great if we could all agree to "celebrate diversity" all the time. But no matter how supportive a multiracial family might be, they still have to live in the world as it is. And that world, unfortunately, is still stained and scarred by racism. In the words of the author (and member of a multiracial family) Jennifer Natalya Fink,

Chapter Four: A Multiracial Life

"You may not believe in race, but race believes in you." That is, even though we know that race is not "real" in the sense that it has no scientific basis, it still has real effects on the way we live every day.

Parents love their kids and want to protect them. So it's natural for parents of every race to wish that "the race talk" could be avoided. It can be especially tough for white parents, who have the privilege of not thinking about race if they don't want to, to understand and help their kids. But experts say that it's important to dive in and have the talk anyway—and not just one talk, many of them.

A study published in the journal *Child Development* found that teaching kids to have pride in their ethnic backgrounds leads to them doing better in school. According to Professor Ming-Te Wang, the author of the study, "when African American parents instill a proud, informed, and sober perspective of race in their sons and daughters, these children are more likely to experience increased academic success." Racial pride has been found to be a very important way to reduce the impact of prejudice on kids.

HOUSEHOLDS WITH PARTNERS OF DIFFERENT RACE OR HISPANIC ORIGIN, BY REGION: 2010

	Partners of different race			Partners of different Hispanic origin		
		Unmarried couples			Unmarried couples	
	Husband and wife	Opposite-sex partners	Same-sex partners	Husband and wife	Opposite-sex partners	Same-sex partners
United States	6.9	14.2	14.5	4.3	8.2	10.4
Northeast	5.3	12.3	12.8	3.2	7.1	8.7
Midwest	4.4	11.1	11.1	2.4	5.4	6.1
South	6.2	12.7	12.1	3.9	7.2	9.2
West	11.6	20.9	20.9	7.5	13.4	15.6

Note: Data are from 2010, before same-sex marriage was legalized nationwide.
Source: U.S. Census Bureau, "Households and Families: 2010", Table 7. https://www.census.gov/prod/cen2010/briefs/c2010br-14.pdf.

Multiracial Families

EMBRACING THE FUTURE

When the Lovings took their stand against prejudice in 1958, an opinion poll showed that only 4 percent of Americans approved of relationships between black and white people. By 2013, that opinion had changed radically. The Gallup polling

Today, an overwhelming percentage of Americans say that they are in favor of multiracial families.

Chapter Four: A Multiracial Life

organization found that 84 percent of Americans approved. Among people aged 18 to 29, approval was at 96 percent—a complete reversal from public opinion in the Lovings' day.

But telling a pollsters that you approve of the *idea* of interracial relationships is one thing. Acting out that approval in real life is something else. The truth is, people in multiracial families still experience prejudice and hard times. Sometimes they have to deal with criticism or insensitive comments from friends, **extended family**, or even total strangers. Biracial kids get asked questions like, "Where are you from?" or "What are you?" Parents who look different from their kids are sometimes confused with nannies or babysitters. Sometimes people even assume these parents have kidnapped their own kids!

Being in a multiracial family has a lot of challenges. But as the numbers of these families increase, we can be optimistic that ignorance will gradually decrease over time. And most people find that standing up to these judgments can make their family stronger and more united than ever.

Text-Dependent Questions

1. What was the "We Are the Fifteen Percent" campaign?
2. What are some of the challenges faced by kids in multiracial families?
3. What is the percentage of people who approve or disapprove of interracial relationships? How has that number changed over time? What do you think this shift means for the future?

Research Project

Is it better to be "color blind" or "color conscious"? Research what experts say, and write an editorial that supports your view.

Multiracial Families

FURTHER READING

Books and Articles

Bishop, Janine. "Adopted." In *East to America: Korean American Life Stories*, edited by Elaine H. Kim and Eui-Young Yu, 306–313. New York: New Press, 1996.

Chang, Sharon H. *Raising Mixed Race: Multiracial Asian Children in a Post-Racial World*. New York: Routledge, 2016.

Fields, Julianna. *Multiracial Families*. Changing Face of Modern Families. Broomall, PA: Mason Crest, 2010.

Gaskins, Pearl Fuyo. *What Are You? Voices of Mixed-Race Young People*. New York: Henry Holt, 1999.

Kaeser, Gigi. *Of Many Colors: Portraits of Multiracial Families*. Amherst: University of Massachusetts Press, 1997.

Online

Belton, Danielle C. "3 Black Adoptees on Racial Identity after Growing Up with White Parents." *The Root*, January 27, 2015. http://www.theroot.com/articles/culture/2015/01/_3_black_adoptees_speak_about_growing_up_with_white_parents.html.

Green, Kristen. "As a White Mom, Helping My Multiracial Kids Feel at Home in Their Skin." NPR, *Code Switch*, July 24, 2015. http://www.npr.org/sections/codeswitch/2015/07/24/419213835/as-a-white-mom-helping-her-multiracial-kids-feel-at-home-in-their-skin.

Race: The Power of an Illusion. Produced by California Newsreel for the Public Broadcasting Service (PBS). http://www.pbs.org/race/000_General/000_00-Home.htm.

Get Help Now

Mixed Heritage Center

The Mixed Heritage Center (MHC) is a clearinghouse of information for people in multiracial families.

http://www.mixedheritagecenter.org

SERIES GLOSSARY

agencies: departments of a government with responsibilities for specific programs.

anxiety: a feeling of worry or nervousness.

biological parents: the woman and man who create a child; they may or not raise it.

caregiving: helping someone with their daily activities.

cognitive: having to do with thinking or understanding.

consensus: agreement among a particular group of people.

custody: legal guardianship of a child.

demographers: people who study information about people and communities.

depression: severe sadness or unhappiness that does not go away easily.

discrimination: singling out a group for unfair treatment.

disparity: a noticeable difference between two things.

diverse: having variety; for example, "ethnically diverse" means a group of people of many different ethnicities.

ethnicity: a group that has a shared cultural heritage.

extended family: the kind of family that includes members beyond just parents and children, such as aunts, uncles, cousins, and so on.

foster care: raising a child (usually temporarily) that is not adopted or biologically yours.

heir: someone who receives another person's wealth and social position after the other person dies.

homogenous: a group of things that are the same.

ideology: a set of ideas and ways of seeing the world.

incarceration: being confined in prison or jail.

inclusive: accepting of everyone.

informally: not official or legal.

Multiracial Families

institution: an established organization, custom, or tradition.

kinship: family relations.

neglect: not caring for something correctly.

patriarchal: a system that is run by men and fathers.

prejudice: beliefs about a person or group based only on simplified and often mistaken ideas.

prevalence: how common a particular trait is in a group of people.

psychological: having to do with the mind.

quantify: to count or measure objectively.

restrictions: limits on what someone can do.

reunification: putting something back together.

secular: nonreligious.

security: being free from danger.

social worker: a person whose job is to help families or children deal with particular problems.

socioeconomic: relating to both social factors (such as race and ethnicity) as well as financial factors (such as class).

sociologists: people who study human society and how it operates.

spectrum: range.

stability: the sense that things will stay the same.

stereotype: a simplified idea about a type of person that is not connected to actual individuals.

stigma: a judgment that something is bad or shameful.

stressor: a situation or event that causes upset (stress).

traumatic: something that's very disturbing and causes long-term damage to a person.

variable: something that can change.

INDEX

Page numbers in *italics* refer to photographs or tables.

adoption
  domestic   13, 28–31
  illegal   32
  international   13, 31–33
  LGBT   *29*
  transracial   12–13, 28, 29–31, 33–35, 38–39
African Americans   23, 28, 33–34, 38, 41
apartheid (South Africa)   *22*, 24
Asian ethnicity   14, 15, 18, 27–28, 38–39
biracial   11, 12, 27, 37, 38, *39*
  challenges   38, 43
Buck, Pearl   *26*, 27–28
Chinese Exclusion Act (1882)   23–24
de Blasio, Bill   *10*, 11
Douglass, Frederick   23
Hispanic ethnicity   12, 14, 28, 33, 41
Indian Child Welfare Act (1978)   34
Loving, Mildred and Richard   *16*, 17–18, 24–25, 42

Loving v. Virginia (1967)   25
McCray, Chirlane   *10*, 11
Multiethnic Placement Act (1994)   30
multiracial families
  advice for   39–40, 41
  celebrities from   13
  numbers of   13–15, 28, 32–33, *34*, *41*
  public opinions on   42–43
National Association of Black Social Workers (NABSW)   33–34
Native American ethnicity   14, 18, 23, 34
Obama, Barack   13
open vs. closed adoptions   29–30
race (concept)   18–19, 20, 21–23
racism   19, 20, 23, 24, 34, 40–41
slavery   19–23
white supremacy   21–24

ABOUT THE AUTHOR

H. W. Poole is a writer and editor of books for young people, including the 13-volume set, *Mental Illnesses and Disorders: Awareness and Understanding* (Mason Crest). She created the *Horrors of History* series (Charlesbridge) and the *Ecosystems* series (Facts On File). She has also been responsible for many critically acclaimed reference books, including *Political Handbook of the World* (CQ Press) and the *Encyclopedia of Terrorism* (SAGE). She was coauthor and editor of *The History of the Internet* (ABC-CLIO), which won the 2000 American Library Association RUSA award.

PHOTO CREDITS

Photos are for illustrative purposes only; individuals depicted are models.
Cover: iStock.com/DragonImages
Dollar Photo Club: 19 william87; 20 Panos
Getty Images: 16 Francis Miller
iStock.com: 6 Mordorlff; 9 Den Kuvaiev; 36 Pamela Moore; 39 IsaacLKoval; 40 Tomwang112
Library of Congress: 23; 26
Shutterstock: 13 Everett Collection; 24 Andy Dean Photography; 29 CREATISTA; 30 DNF Style; 34 Varina and Jay Patel; 42 logoboom